Original title:
When You're Not Sure, Just Dance

Copyright © 2025 Creative Arts Management OÜ
All rights reserved.

Author: Julian Prescott
ISBN HARDBACK: 978-1-80566-023-1
ISBN PAPERBACK: 978-1-80566-318-8

A Symphony of Uncertainty

Offbeat steps in silly shoes,
Twists and turns, what's there to lose?
Clumsy laughter fills the air,
Follow the rhythm, without a care.

Mirror ball spins a wild show,
Wobble left, then pirouette slow.
The band plays tunes from left field,
With every misstep, boldness is revealed.

Curves of Courage

Belly flops on a dance floor bright,
Gyrate with glee; it's pure delight.
A cha-cha cha with a goofy grin,
Even if you wobble, let the fun begin!

Swirl like a tornado, let's go for a ride,
With questionable moves, let joy be your guide.
Heels over head, in high fashion pose,
Confidence blooms, as the laughter grows.

The Dance of Decisions

Step left, now step to the right,
Spin like a top, then hold on tight.
With each decision, do a jig,
Might look absurd, but man, it's big!

Flap your arms, start a conga line,
No wrong or right, just feel divine.
Over the top with a cartwheel flair,
Who cares if you fall? Get up, don't despair!

Unpredictable Rhythms

Shake a leg, do the chicken dance,
Twist and twirl, take a crazy chance.
The clock ticks funny, but who cares now?
Bounce to the beat, just take a bow!

Hiccups in timing, like a silly song,
Fumble your way, you can't go wrong.
Laugh it off in this whimsical trance,
Life's a party; let's all prance!

Feet That Fear Nothing

Wobble like a jelly, unsteady on my toes,
Twirl and trip through laughter, that's how confidence grows.
A misstep to the left, and then I shake it right,
All the world's a stage, and I'm the star tonight.

Funky chicken flapping, arms out like a kite,
Each awkward little jiggle is a pure delight.
So take my hand, my friend, let's bust a wild move,
With every silly shuffle, we'll find a way to groove.

Chaotic Waltz of Doubt

Two left feet in tandem, they lead me to the door,
But every spin and tumble opens up new floor.
A tango with uncertainty, I stumble and I slide,
The rhythm of confusion gives my worries a ride.

Grin like a fool while I twirl and sway,
Who needs a plan? Just twist and play!
Fumble like a clown, but don't let it weigh,
In this dizzy dance-off, we'll both find our way.

Move with the Breeze

Float like a feather, bob like a balloon,
Not a care in the world, just humming a tune.
The wind tickles my cheeks as I swing side to side,
Every little movement feels like a joyride.

Glide with grace, or trip over a shoe,
Laughing all the way, it's the best thing to do.
The secret's in the wobbles and the giggles that lend,
So let's dance like the daffodils, my funny friend.

Freedom in Each Step

Heel-to-toe and then whoops! Here we go again,
Eccentric pirouettes, don't know when to end.
With every silly shuffle, I escape the mundane,
Each step is a freedom, I'll dance through the rain.

Ballet of blunders, a shuffle of glee,
Let's find our wild rhythm, just you wait and see.
Twist your worries away, just follow my lead,
In this wacky movement, we'll both be set free!

Rhythms of Uncertainty

Wobbling hips in a crowded room,
Two left feet chasing shadows' gloom.
A chicken strut, a wild flair,
Should I laugh, or do I care?

Spinning in a dizzy haze,
Lost in unplanned, funny ways.
A toe taps out a quirky beat,
Life's a party, feel the heat!

Twirling like a bag of chips,
Making friends with all my slips.
Laughter echoes, spirits soar,
Who needs rhythm? Let's explore!

With every jiggle, every twirl,
I leap into the cosmic swirl.
So here's to chaos, jumps, and prance,
Because we're all just winging chance!

Letting Go in Motion

A shuffle here, a wiggle there,
What's this move? I do declare!
A flop and flop, I slide and sway,
Let's pretend it's part of the play.

With flailing arms and spinning feet,
In the spotlight, life's a treat.
Jelly legs on a coffee spree,
Oh, look! A dance-off just for me!

A misstep here, a laugh erupts,
Oh, my goodness, how it disrupts!
The rhythm's off, but spirits high,
Who needs direction? Let's just fly!

With silly grins and joyful cries,
We'll dance beneath the slanting skies.
Embrace the giggle, let it show,
Life's a dance, just let it flow!

Steps into the Unknown

A hop, a skip, what's this I feel?
A beat that seems to roll and reel.
My foot's leading, doing its own,
In this chaos, I have grown.

With every twist, a grin appears,
Not just from steps but from wild cheers.
Crashing into laughter's sound,
In every blunder, joy is found.

A dance of doubts, let's take the stage,
Every flub turns a brand new page.
Why worry now? Just give a whirl,
Life's the dance, give it a twirl!

Stumbling forward, backward, too,
Inventing moves—yes, that's what we do!
A boogie down the uncertain lane,
Here's our anthem to misstep's gain!

Twirls of Ambiguity

Oh, the beauty in every twist,
Flailing limbs? Oh wait, a missed.
Bouncing here, gliding there,
In every fumble, love is rare!

With a spin that brings out the giggle,
Life's like this quirky wiggle.
Trust your feet to lead you right,
In the silly, find delight!

Each stumble is a step to grace,
A comical dance in open space.
As laughter leads, we twirl around,
In the nonsense, joy is found.

So when in doubt, just sway with glee,
Dance your way through the mystery.
For in these spins and light-hearted prance,
We discover magic in the chance!

Swaying Through the Ambiguity

Wobbling like a jelly, oh what a sight,
Feet shuffled left, then right, what a delight!
Bumping into shadows, laughing at fate,
In the chaos we dance, don't hesitate!

With twirls and spins, we embrace the mess,
Fumbling through moves but feeling no stress,
A laugh in each stumble, a giggle in falls,
Swaying through life's dance, hear the laughter calls!

Hazy Horizons

Out on the floor, my mind feels so hazy,
Forgotten the steps, but I still feel crazy,
Bumping with strangers, we dance and collide,
In this foggy groove, let chuckles decide!

The lights blur around, quite the dazzling dance,
Whirling like a kite, caught in romance,
With every wrong turn, a grin on my face,
In this dazed little waltz, I've found my own place!

Bright Beats

Bass dropping heavy, a beat that won't stop,
In this corner, I trip, in that one, I hop,
Laugh lines expanding with every misstep,
On this wild rhythm, the world takes a rep!

With sparkles and giggles, we twirl through the night,
Feet finding the groove, oh, what a delight,
Who cares if we fumble? I'll swing with the flow,
In this carnival dance, let the good vibes grow!

Celebrate the Confusion

In this confetti storm, we lose all control,
Two left feet tango, it's good for the soul,
With hiccups and giggles, we twist and we twirl,
Celebrating the chaos, come on, give it a whirl!

Jiggle and jive, with no time to pout,
Bumbling through spins, there's no room for doubt,
Hands in the air, watch the worries all flee,
In the heart of the madness, we dance wild and free!

Shuffling Through Life

Life's a big party, where laughter rings clear,
With shuffles and slides, let go of all fear,
A hop to the left and a wiggle to right,
We'll dance to the beats, under soft city light!

Each twist tells a story, of falling and laughs,
Sharing the love through these bumpy paths,
With faces aglow, life's a comedy show,
As we sway through the shuffle, let your spirit glow!

Freestyle Flights of Fancy

Twist and twirl, you're feeling bold,
Flap your arms, let stories unfold.
Skip like a squirrel, hop like a flea,
Who knew a dance could set you free?

Laughter bubbles like a fizzy drink,
With every jig, discover and think.
Feet may stumble, but spirits soar,
In this hop, life's never a bore.

Giddy spins and silly jumps,
Close your eyes, just feel the thumps.
Curly locks and mismatched socks,
Become the star on your own blocks.

Wobble like jelly, bounce like a ball,
Embrace the rhythm, surrender to the call.
Whirl around, break the mundane,
In this frolic, there's no shame!

The Cha-Cha of Possibilities

Step to the left, then shake it right,
Life's a dance, oh what a sight!
Clap your hands, make some noise,
Mix it up, with joy deploys!

Slip on bananas, take a chance,
Twirl like you're caught in a trance.
Swaying hips and silly grins,
Every cha-cha, adventure begins.

Sashay past doubt, let worries fall,
With each new step, let's have a ball.
Forget the script, it's not a test,
In this dance, just be your best!

Tango with courage, groove with glee,
Nothing matters but being free.
Leap to the beat, don't say no,
In this cha-cha, let yourself glow!

Sway with the Serendipity

Catch the rhythm in the air,
Dance like no one's anywhere.
Swirl with laughter, spin with grace,
Find the joy in every place.

Tumble down the hill, don't mind the grass,
A pirouette, what a classy pass!
Chasing clouds, or pouncing puddles,
Embrace the giggles amidst the muddles.

Shuffle to the left, then to the right,
Every misstep ignites the night.
Make a fool, and own the stage,
In this tango, forget your age.

Serendipity knocks on your door,
Step inside, hear the laughter roar!
Tonight we sway, we laugh, we play,
In this dance, forever stay!

Boogie Beneath the Clouds

Under the sky, let's bust a move,
With floppy hats, we find our groove.
Fingers snap and elbows fly,
In this boogie, let out a sigh!

Rain or shine, we'll shimmy along,
Every bit of laughter is a joyful song.
Wearing mismatched shoes, feeling grand,
Every twirl is an artwork planned.

Skateboard tricks and cartwheel flips,
Hiccups bring giggles, laughter trips.
Stomp like a dinosaur, bounce like a bee,
This boogie beneath the clouds feels free.

Oh, grab a friend, share the beat,
Feel the warmth beneath your feet.
With disco balls or just your soul,
In this dance, we become whole!

Steps with a Side of Spontaneity

In socks that slide across the floor,
I twirl and spin, who could ask for more?
The cat looks on with judging eyes,
But I'm the star in this wild surprise.

A misstep here, a stumble there,
I laugh out loud, without a care.
The kitchen's now a ballroom wide,
Where laughter's rhythm cannot hide.

Finding Solace in Motion

The world outside is full of fuss,
So I shake my hips, who needs a bus?
With every twirl, my worries fade,
In my little dance, life's joy is made.

I jump and jiggle, a noodle gone wild,
With every beat, I'm forever a child.
The neighbors peek, their brows in a frown,
But I'm the king of this carefree town.

The Freedom to Fall

I trip like a toddler, flat on my face,
Yet giggles erupt, I'm winning this race.
With arms flailing wide, I take to the air,
Who needs coordination? I haven't a care.

I roll and I tumble, in fits of glee,
Every fall is a dance move, just wait and see!
A leap to the left, then a slide to the right,
Every misstep feels so terribly right.

Whirl of Whimsy

Under the glow of the kitchen light,
I dance with a broom, it's such a delight.
The dust bunnies join in this jovial spree,
With twirls and giggles, I'm happy and free.

In mismatched socks, I take the lead,
My audience? Just me, and my dog, indeed!
We whirl and we twirl, through laughter and cheer,
In this wacky ballet, I have nothing to fear.

Dance of the Discoverers

In socks that slip upon the floor,
We twirl and spin, always wanting more.
With bumping elbows, we laugh and jive,
Each misstep proves we're truly alive.

Our feet go left, then wildly right,
Like tangled yarn in a cat's delight.
The beat goes on, the music's loud,
We bust a move, attracting a crowd.

Fusion of Fate and Fancy

A jig in rainboots, slippery and bright,
Who knew my shoes could cause such fright?
But with every twist, I shake off my fear,
Just wait 'til you see my next career!

The cat meows, as if to say,
'That's not how you should dance today!'
Yet here I am, with arms out wide,
Embracing chaos, my silly pride.

Pathways Unpredictable

The floor is lava; hop, skip, and sway,
In this bizarre game we play today.
With every shuffle, a giggle erupts,
As clumsy feet cause us all to corrupt.

The walls must be jealous of our great moves,
As we swirl around like erratic grooves.
Slipping and sliding across the room,
We chuckle and spin, shaking off gloom.

Journey of Stray Steps

Oh look, a grand leap, oh what a sight!
Into the chair that's not quite right!
With laughter bouncing off every wall,
We wiggle and giggle, embracing the fall.

The dog thinks we're nuts, woofing away,
As we prance and pirouette in pure disarray.
But with each flounder, the joy multiplies,
For in silly moments, our spirit flies!

Groovy Resilience

In a world that's spinning mad,
I stumble, trip, then start to glad.
With two left feet, I find my way,
In this groovy mess, I laugh and sway.

The floor is mine, or so I claim,
With jigs that could put pros to shame.
I shimmy past my doubt and fear,
A dance like this? It's worth a cheer!

The music's wild, the lights are bright,
I twirl like noodles, hold on tight.
In every slip, a chance to learn,
With every spin, I start to turn.

So let the rhythm lead the way,
A funny jig for a wobbly day.
With laughter shared, I find my groove,
Resilience found in every move.

Uncertain Symphony

A beat drops in, but I'm unsure,
Do I go left or twirl some more?
With feet like jelly, I take a leap,
In this funny play, no time for sleep.

The music plays a curious song,
I swing and sway, can't go too wrong.
A bump, a bash, a giggle too,
This uncertain dance, my funky debut!

Like a marionette with a snappy twist,
I fumble, tumble, but can't resist.
With every shake, my worries erase,
I laugh at the chaos, embrace the pace.

So let's not fret, let's just be free,
In this wild symphony, just you and me.
With every misstep, a joy we'll find,
Uncertain moves can be so refined!

Rhythm of the Heart's Query

My heart beats quick in a curious spree,
Do I step right or left—oh who could see?
With twirls of doubt and hops of glee,
    I wonder if this dance reflects me.

A shake of hips, a flutter of toes,
The rhythm stumbles, but that's how it goes.
I question, I wiggle, my spirit's out loud,
In this ridiculous jig, I'm part of the crowd.

Each beat a riddle, each pause a tease,
I'll shuffle along, do what I please.
In laughter and folly, I lose all stares,
Every quirky step? A joy that declares!

So come take my hand, let's query the dance,
With hearts at the helm, we'll leap and prance.
In this laughter-laden rhythm, no need to debate,
Let's dance through the puzzlement, isn't it great?

Trusting the Tangle

In the twisty turns of a fancy step,
I'm tied in knots—what's next? A rep?
With giggles spilling like candy cane,
I embrace the tangle, I'll not complain.

My feet have minds of their own tonight,
A salsa with sprinkles, silly and bright.
As I spin and laugh, it feels so right,
Trusting the chaos, what a delight!

A wobble, a jig, oh, where do I go?
The dance floor's alive, putting on quite a show.
With every misstep, my confidence grows,
A funny ballet where anything goes!

So rise with the music, let's sway and twine,
In this tangle we dance, it's perfectly fine.
Laughter's our partner, just let it enhance,
In trusting the tangle, we find our chance!

Steps Beyond the Shadows

In the corner, doubts do creep,
But on the floor, I take a leap.
Shuffle left and twirl away,
Who needs a map when you can sway?

Laughing at my clumsy feet,
Stumbling, but I can't be beat.
Every misstep, a brand-new chance,
To wiggle, jiggle, laugh, and dance.

The lights may flicker, don't you frown,
Just throw your arms and spin around.
With each step, my worries fade,
In this silly, joyful parade.

So here I go, I'll shake it loose,
An awkward move, but what's the use?
With every giggle, I break the trance,
Life's a carnival, come join the dance!

Rhythm of the Undecided

Twirling thoughts, a merry mess,
Should I stay or just confess?
The beat drops low, my heart's a drum,
Why not shimmy? Here I come!

A hesitant tap, then a full-on glide,
Uncertainty turns to silly pride.
Shake those worries left and right,
In this chaos, everything feels right.

The crowd is watching, what a sight,
A tango with my inner fright.
Flipping flops, it's quite absurd,
But laughter echoes, oh, haven't you heard?

So dance with me, let's take a chance,
On silly moves and a goofy stance.
With each misstep, my heart will see,
The joy in dancing, wild and free!

Let the Music Guide You

A tune that calls, it pulls me near,
I'm lost in rhythm, have no fear.
One foot forward, then I slip,
A little waltz turns into a trip.

Cackling as I miss a beat,
Who knew that tripping could be sweet?
The notes can guide this hapless fool,
In this dance, I find my groove, my rule.

With a pop, a hop, and a sway,
Not quite sure, but I'll display.
Fumbling steps and friendly grins,
In this chaos, the laughter wins.

The dance floor's bright, my spirit's high,
Just let the music tell me why.
With every chuckle, we all advance,
In this crazy life, let's take a chance!

A Leap into the Unknown

Wobbly knees, but here I go,
Into the rhythm, I'll steal the show.
A little twist, and what's this flare?
Can't resist the step of dare!

Friends are giggling, but who's to judge?
A moonwalk here, I'll give a nudge.
The floor is slick, my shoes are tight,
But in this whirl, I feel just right.

I spin and twirl, a dizzy whirl,
With mischief's grace, I start to twirl.
Laughter bubbles, can't contain,
This joyous dance that ends the strain.

So leap with me, into the light,
Embrace the unknown, hold on tight.
In every stumble, joy is found,
Together we'll make silly sounds!

Spin with the Unknown

Twist and twirl in a wobbly way,
Your feet may slip, but hey, hooray!
With every stumble, a giggle will rise,
Who knew confusion could be such a prize?

Round and round like a dizzy kite,
Laugh at your shadow, it's quite a sight.
The floor is your friend, not a foe in disguise,
Just boogie along with starry-eyed sighs.

Forget the steps, they don't have a clue,
Just follow that feeling, not one, but a few.
With mischief in mind and a sprightly cheer,
Dance like the world is your stage, my dear!

So spin and sway without a care,
Happy accidents make the best flair.
Let rhythm's riddle wrap you tight,
In the joyful whirl of your own limelight.

Pulse of the Perplexed

Bouncing like beans in a cartoon frame,
Each awkward move is part of the game.
Heartbeats quicken, no map to unfold,
In this clumsy chaos, let stories be told.

Your shoes may squeak, your shirt might twist,
Yet every blunder's a moment not missed.
With laughter that bubbles and tickles the air,
You shimmy and shake without a single care.

Step on your toes? Give it a spin!
Dance like you mean it, let giggles begin.
The beat's a riddle, a puzzle to tease,
Just throw in some jazz and truly appease.

So waltz through confusion with style and flair,
Look around you—are they all aware?
Embrace the chaos, let each moment glance,
The best kind of magic is born of mischance!

Boundless Beats

Jumping jacks turned into moonwalks,
Rhythms can giggle and even talk.
In every flop and unexpected glide,
A burst of joy cannot be denied.

Swim like a fish, or hop like a frog,
Your body's an enigma wrapped in a smog.
Bumping and grinding, no need to be neat,
The floor's just a canvas beneath your two feet.

Forget perfection, let go of the norms,
In this bizarre dance, imagination storms.
Let your spirit burst forth with each funny twist,
'Cause every small victory's worth being kissed.

With arms flailing wide, and a chuckle or two,
You're the star of a show that's both wild and new.
So sway with abandon, and hold on to glee,
In this world of movement, you're perfectly free!

In the Arms of Ambiguity

Flop like a fish, then swagger like a cat,
Dancing in circles, what's wrong with that?
The rhythm's uncertain; your style's a delight,
Each jive and jolt feels just so right.

With smiles erupting at every odd turn,
You laugh at the questions you didn't discern.
A bump, a slide, two left feet in play,
The dance floor's a circus, come join the array!

With a wiggle and nod, let the fun navigate,
Mistakes are just tickets—don't hesitate!
So plunge into mirth, leave wisdom behind,
In the arms of confusion, new treasures you'll find.

Celebrate each quirk, let your spirit unfurl,
For dancing is laughter—let joy do a whirl.
As rhythms collide, be bold in your stance,
A whimsical journey, just take a chance!

Pirouettes of Possibility

In a world so vast and wide,
We twirl with glee, let's set aside.
A slip, a spin, a laugh so loud,
We flip our doubts, we're feeling proud.

With socks on floors, we take a chance,
Who knew the kitchen's good for dance?
But watch that cat, oh what a sight,
He's joining in, he's feeling bright.

The fridge becomes our greatest stage,
With every step, we break the cage.
Miscalled the tune? Just laugh it off,
The rhythm's here; just give a scoff.

So twirl away, spin wild and free,
In every glance, there's comedy.
With silly moves and goofy grins,
We dance through chaos and let light in.

Unscripted Steps of Life

The music starts; we feel the beat,
We throw our hands, we stomp our feet.
No script to follow, we just pretend,
Each step a giggle, each twist a friend.

Like penguins waddling in a race,
We find our joy in every space.
A misstep here, a fun-filled fall,
Who needs perfection? We'll have a ball!

With popcorn flies and frozen fries,
We dance like no one's 'round to spy.
A leap, a hop; we lose control,
The laughter echoes, warms the soul.

So swing away with all your pride,
Life's choreographed in joyful stride.
Forget the rules; just feel the zest,
In unscripted steps, we are the best!

Groove with the Unfamiliar

In strange shoes, we bounce and sway,
Exploring grooves in our own way.
A jazz hand here, a twist of fate,
Funky moves can't wait; we're late!

With each mistake, we burst with cheer,
A practiced step? Oh, never fear!
We'll shimmy close with noodle arms,
Just watch the world respond to charms!

The awkward pauses life can send,
Turn into dance; they're all our friends.
A flick of hips, a pop of toes,
We'll leap over our everyday woes.

So bring your flair, your quirkiest shoes,
Let rhythm wake up sleepy blues.
In unfamiliar lands, we'll find our vibe,
With every shuffle, we're a lively tribe!

Merging Hearts and Hesitations

With every heartbeat, we may stumble,
Yet in this dance, we will not grumble.
A hesitant step leads to a grin,
You can't resist, let chaos in!

We sway like jelly, and that's just fine,
Each sway reveals a special sign.
Life's little hiccups, we just embrace,
As laughter bounces through the space.

So take my hand; let's lose the fear,
In twirls and spins, we'll both endear.
For when we meet in awkward thrills,
The joy erupts, the laughter spills.

With merging hearts, the rhythm calls,
And in the chaos, love enthralls.
So dance with me, no judgment here,
In every hesitation, let's cheer!

Spirals of Spontaneity

In the kitchen, I twirl with delight,
The cat jumps, thinks I'm a fright.
My socks are mismatched, oh what a sight,
But the music's so loud, I feel just right.

I trip on the rug, do an awkward spin,
Last week's leftovers stuck to my chin.
Neighbors peek out, confused where I've been,
But the beat calls me back, let the chaos begin!

With spatula in hand, I wave like a queen,
The dance of the dinner, my jiving routine.
The dog howls along, if you know what I mean,
In this kitchen ballet, I'm just a machine.

So laugh as I spin, let's all be absurd,
In a world full of rules, let's twist and be blurred.
With every misstep, I'm just being stirred,
In this silly dance life, I'm totally inferred.

Unraveling with Every Turn

In the grocery aisle, I make my brave stand,
While dodging the carts, the spins aren't quite planned.
I shuffle with veggies, but still feel quite grand,
A pirouette, and I drop a ripe plum from my hand.

The old lady chuckles, she thinks it's a show,
I wink and I whirl, let my wildness flow.
With a cart full of snacks, I'm the star of the row,
In this here ballet, I'm all set to glow.

The peanut butter jar is my partner, so fun,
With a jig and a laugh, we dance 'til we're done.
A hit and a giggle, two-stepping and run,
With each twist and turn, chaos has begun.

As the checkout line waits, I bust out the flair,
Coupons in hand, dancing without a care.
Life's just a party, and laughter fills the air,
So grab your groove, and dance anywhere!

Calibrate Your Cadence

On the work desk, I add some flair,
While spreadsheets are calling, I dance in midair.
I knock over pens, but I do not despair,
With a shimmy and shake, I breathe in the flair.

The boss walks on by, looking quite stern,
But I pivot and twirl, watch that frown take a turn.
A giggle escapes, and oh, how I yearn,
To make every meeting a fun place to burn.

The printer's now jamming, it's giving me sass,
But I leap over wires, like a pro with sass.
With a paper airplane, watch it fly and pass,
In this wild workplace, I'll dance with class.

So if you feel stuck, just sway in your seat,
Let the rhythm of chaos make life feel complete.
Dance through the deadlines, create your own beat,
In a world full of work, find your groove sweet.

Footsteps in Flux

At the park in the rain, I splash in the mud,
With leaps and with bounds, I'm a giggling bud.
Umbrellas are bobbing, like flowers in flood,
I dance through the puddles, embracing the crud.

The squirrels look puzzled, as I spin 'round a tree,
Their chittering echoes, is it all meant for me?
While parents just sigh, and roll eyes with glee,
My two-legged ballet is fierce and carefree.

Each step's a surprise, with a jump or a glide,
I laugh with the wind, casting worries aside.
Even clouds can't dim this joyful ride,
For every odd shuffle, there's no need to hide.

So take off your shoes, feel the earth in your feel,
Let go of your worries, unleash your wild zeal.
In a world of confusion, just dance, let it heal,
With footsteps in flux, life's joy you'll reveal.

The Dance of Possibilities

In fluffy socks, we take the floor,
With twirls and spins, we beg for more.
A misstep here, a stumble there,
Laughter erupts, it's all a fair.

On tippy toes, we reach for dreams,
While giggling at our wobbly schemes.
The music plays, our worries fade,
In this wild act, we're all displayed.

So come on now, let's shake it loose,
We'll dance like clowns, no need for a truce.
A shimmy, a shake, we'll take the chance,
In silly steps, we find our dance.

With every beat, our fumbles gleam,
We laugh so hard, we almost scream.
In this ballet of the whacky heart,
The dance of life, a funny art.

Motion in the Mist

Through swirling fog, we sway and sway,
Is this a dance or just dismay?
With arms flailing in the misty air,
We search for rhythm, unaware.

The moonlight glints on shoes so bright,
As we two-step into the night.
With every twist, we lose our way,
In this motion, we choose to play.

Invisible walls, we bump and glide,
In this unclear dance, we take our pride.
A cha-cha skipped, a slide gone wrong,
In the misty haze, we hum our song.

Whirls of laughter, we'll dance till dawn,
With each misstep, a new giggle's born.
Embrace the blur, let yourself unfurl,
In the misty haze, let laughter whirl.

Unscripted Moments

Life's a stage where plans go wrong,
We dance along to a silly song.
A pirouette becomes a flop,
Yet up we rise, we cannot stop.

An awkward glance and a funky twist,
In these moments, we can't resist.
The music skips, but we don't care,
In these unscripted ways, we dare.

With every spin, a comic flair,
Our goofy moves become the air.
Like marionettes with tangled strings,
We laugh so hard, our joy just springs.

This is the dance of chance and fun,
The rhythm finds us, two as one.
So take the stage and lose your fear,
In unscripted times, the joy is clear.

Grooves in the Gray

In shades of gray, we stomp and slide,
With splats of joy, we cannot hide.
Our limbs are loose, our hearts are light,
In this quirky dance, we take flight.

With rubbery legs and crazy moves,
We'll shake the gloom, we'll find the grooves.
In every giggle, a spark ignites,
Grooves in the gray chase off the frights.

A shuffle here, a jive, a twirl,
We lose ourselves in this dance whirl.
The beats collide with laughter's cheer,
In every awkward moment, we persevere.

So join the fun, let worries fade,
In timeless grooves, we feel remade.
With every bounce in this odd ballet,
We light the world in shades of gray.

Sashay into the Mist

In the fog, I'll take a spin,
With a wiggle and a grin.
Twirl and twist through hazy air,
Laughing hard, without a care.

Nose to nose with doubts so bright,
I cha-cha with all my might.
With each step, I trip and slip,
But I can't resist this funny trip.

Twirling round, I start to flail,
Dancing like a wind-blown sail.
Giggling at my silly plight,
In this fog, I'll dance all night.

Foggy feet, don't hide your flair,
Sashay with style, show you dare.
Mist or not, I own my show,
In the haze, I steal the glow.

A Jive with Anxiety

Bouncing beats in my head,
While I do the dancy dread.
Jiving with my racing thoughts,
But my feet tie simple knots.

Every shuffle feels like flight,
Yet I'm grounded, what a sight!
With a wiggle, shake the fear,
Groove away, the end is near.

Round and round, my heart's a drum,
Dancing wild, then feeling glum.
But oh, look! A laugh appears,
Jiving joys through all the tears.

In the spotlight, I let it loose,
Twists and turns, what's the use?
Swing and sway, release the fright,
Together we'll dance through the night.

Two Left Feet, One Brave Heart

Two left feet, but brave as day,
In my dance, I find my way.
Stumbling along, what a sight,
Every misstep feels so right.

With a hop, I leap for joy,
Like a clumsy, goofy boy.
Laughing loud, despite the fall,
Maybe I'm the best of all!

Hands out wide, let laughter flow,
For who cares if I don't know?
Spinning in my silly style,
Every wobble brings a smile.

One brave heart, I face the floor,
Joyful chaos, I adore.
Two left feet but soul set free,
Come and dance along with me!

Whirls Among the What-ifs

In the swirl of what could be,
I spin and twirl, quite carefree.
Dizziness in every turn,
With a giggle, I just yearn.

Each "what-if" like a passing breeze,
Tickles me; oh, such a tease!
I leap and flutter, round and round,
Daring laughter to be found.

Questions chase, like shadows flee,
But my dance sets my mind free.
I pirouette through all the doubt,
Knocking fears, that's what it's about.

Every step, a chance to dare,
Whirls among the what-ifs air.
Living life with joyful glee,
In this chaos, I find me!

Spiral into the Unexpected

Twisting and turning, oops, I'm a mess,
Step on a foot, what a dance test!
Grinning at chaos with a quirky smile,
Who knew flailing could be such a style?

A wiggle, a jiggle, and then I slip,
Stirring the laughter, let's take a trip.
With each little stumble, joy starts to spark,
Dancing like no one's home, igniting the dark.

The tune may be silly, the rhythm bizarre,
I spin like a top, then fly like a star.
Each wave of the hand is a story untold,
In this carnival chaos, I'm brave and bold!

So here's to the moments that make us trip,
To every odd twirl and inebriated flip.
We'll twine in the giggles and let our hearts cheer,
For life's best cha-cha's are born from good cheer!

Untamed But Alive

My feet are wild, they dance on their own,
Tripping on toes, I'm the clumsy but known.
With every misstep, I take off in flight,
Flailing and laughing well into the night.

The beat keeps on pulsing, my heart's in a whirl,
Spinning like a whirlwind, what a great twirl!
Arms up to the ceiling, let's give it a twang,
Forget about grace, let the laughter hang.

Around I go, in loops and in bends,
Meeting the sofa, where my dance ends.
But fear not, dear folks, for the fun's only begun,
In this wild dance-off, we're all number one!

So join in the jigs, the fandango of fate,
Let's unshackle our spirits, it's never too late.
With each laugh and stumble, delight we shall find,
For untamed and messy is genuinely kind!

A Celebration of Missteps

Here's to the stumbles, the bumbles, the falls,
A festival of folly, let's answer the calls!
We'll cha-cha on crumples and swagger on slips,
To the rhythm of laughter, we'll dance with our quips.

With two left feet, how can we go wrong?
The beat is so catchy, let's boogie along!
A high-kick, a fumble, then oops, what a sight,
In the land of the silly, we twirl into light.

The spotlight's a beacon for flops of all kinds,
Critics are absent, only joy intertwines.
Egos at rest, we'll shimmy with glee,
In this wacky parade, we all can be free!

So bring on the fails, we'll toast to the grace,
With slip-ups and giggles, we'll conquer this space.
For every misstep is a chance to romance,
In this clumsy ballet, let's take one more chance!

Dance of the Serendipitous

Waltzing through life with a tiptoe or two,
Finding the rhythm in things we can't view.
A hop and a skip, oh look, there's my shoe!
Let's jiggle right past as the laughter ensues.

Twist to the left, then a lurch to the right,
What's that I stumbled on? Is it day, is it night?
A hopscotch of fate, we'll clamor and cheer,
For the best little dances are born from good cheer.

Oh look, here comes chaos with jello-like moves,
A dance of the unexpected grooves in the grooves.
With each blooper and blunder, we create a new tune,
For mischief is magic when it's made by the moon.

So let's gather our friends, and with whimsy let's prance,
In the festival of flailing, we give it a chance.
Each shuffle and shuffle, in a jubilant spree,
In the dance of the lucky, just happy to be!

Rhythmic Revelations

In a room full of socks and old shoes,
I twirl like a twinkling star,
With a jig from the fridge to my socks,
Feeling quite bizarre!

My cat judges my every move,
As I kick and I spin,
But nothing beats the groove,
Let the comedy begin!

I've got two left feet, but who cares?
I'll shake like a jelly bean,
In a world of fancy layers,
I'm the dancing queen!

So if you see me wobble, laugh and grin,
I'm here to spread some cheer,
With each slip and trip, I'm born again,
Let's dance away our fear!

Dancing in the Fog

The floor is slippery with peanut butter,
My moves are, well, a sight to see,
I'm grooving like a confused otter,
In a fog of my own decree!

I wave my arms like a windmill,
Footloose in my bubble of bliss,
Who needs grace? I'm fueled by thrill,
Every slip is a dance floor kiss!

A jig in the kitchen, I spill some tea,
My partner's a mop, but that's okay,
With a twirl and a spin, it's just you and me,
In this fog, let's dance all day!

The neighbors peek through their blinds,
With laughter and shaking heads,
But I'm lost in my joyful finds,
Wearing my socks like threads!

Footloose in the Abyss

In the valley of mismatched shoes,
I leap over dust and old grime,
With each clumsy pivot I choose,
I'm transcending the limits of time!

The abyss is my disco floor,
Where shadows dance with glee,
I might trip, but I'll ask for more,
As I waddle like a jubilee!

With laughter echoing all around,
I spin like a whirling dervish,
My balance? It's never found,
But my spirit's too vicious!

Who knew the void could be this bright?
With joy dripping like melting ice,
In this darkness, I find my light,
Let's dance, let's roll the dice!

Jubilant Ignorance

With a grin and a goofy stance,
I leap into the unknown,
Who cares if I can't find my balance,
I've got my heart as a microphone!

A party where rules are all broken,
I twist like a noodle, so silly,
With bursts of laughter, the unspoken,
Becomes my favorite filly!

Twirling down the hallway, I fly,
Chasing shadows, I lose my way,
But joy is my ever-ready tie,
Together, we'll play all day!

In a world where logic is shy,
I flail with glorious delight,
Who knows when or how or why,
But let's dance into the night!

Shake Off the Hesitation

Wiggle your toes, let them groove,
Shake off the fear, find your move.
Spin like a top, take a chance,
Life's a stage, so start your dance.

Shake your hips, let laughter win,
Twirl those worries, where to begin?
Step to the left, then to the right,
In this moment, everything's bright.

Jive with the clouds, jump with the breeze,
Forget your troubles, do as you please.
Grab your friends, join the fun,
Life's like a party, we've just begun!

So lose your mind, let your heart race,
Waltz through the chaos, find your place.
With every step, melt down the walls,
In this silly dance, humor calls.

Footloose in Doubt

Flap like a chicken, strut like a peacock,
Embrace the rhythm, tick like a clock.
Every misstep might bring a cheer,
Twisting through life with a grin and a sneer.

Skip over puddles, bounce in the rain,
Crafting a story, dancing through pain.
With every stumble, let laughter unfold,
Footloose in doubt, be brave, be bold.

Chuckle and wiggle, shake off the gloom,
Dive into chaos, bloom like a bloom.
The dance floor awaits with a wink and a sway,
Dance like a jester, let worries decay.

Then leap through the air like a gummy bear,
Living in laughter, life's a fair.
Every jiggle brings joy to your heart,
In this wacky journey, we'll never part.

The Tango of Tomorrow

Two left feet, but oh what flair,
Trip on my toes, fly through the air.
With every misstep, my heart claps loud,
In this tango of life, I'm feeling proud.

Spin with the shadows, dip with the light,
Laugh at the moments that tickle the night.
Step on toes, but dance with the soul,
In this ballet of chaos, we're always whole.

Slides and twirls, here comes the twist,
Joyfully tangle, we can't resist.
Tomorrow's the stage with rooms so bright,
Embrace the absurd, dance day and night.

So grab a partner, take them along,
In this quirky duet, we can't go wrong.
Life's just a dance, so shake off the sorrow,
With every shimmy, we'll craft tomorrow.

Leap into the Unknown

Jump like a frog, leap like a bean,
The dance floor whispers, come join the scene.
Dare to be silly, forget what's planned,
Embrace the madness, take a stand.

Somersault through thoughts, wiggle with glee,
Twisting and turning, just let it be.
Shuffle your feet, let your hair fly,
In this odd ballet, we'll kiss the sky.

With every twist, we're chasing the thrill,
Roll with the punches, dance at will.
Laughter erupts like bubbles in soda,
In this zany groove, feel the euphoria.

Bow to the silly, leap and abide,
In the wild unknown, let joy be your guide.
With wobbly moves, we'll find the flow,
In this dance of life, let your spirit glow.

Vulnerable Pirouettes

Twirl around, whoops, there goes my shoe,
Caught in the moment, can't help but stew.
Spinning like a top, I stumble and sway,
Laughing at myself, come what may.

Full of grace but with a twist,
Every misstep adds to the list.
Ballet slippers stuck on the floor,
Dance like nobody's keeping score.

A leap of faith, or was it a flop?
Somersault dreams make my heart stop.
With giggles escaping, I take a bow,
Vulnerable pirouettes, oh wow!

So here I go, in a quirky trance,
Hoping for magic with this wild dance.
Swinging like a pendulum, too much glee,
What a splendid sight, just look at me!

Mysterious Steps

With every beat, a riddle unfolds,
A shuffle here, where the story holds.
Mystery in motion, lost in a spin,
What's next, my friend? Come join in the din.

Sideways glances, and then a twirl,
Someone's hiccup turns into a whirl.
Each funky move is a secret hinted,
In the dance floor shadows, we're all minted.

Can you hear the whispers in the air?
As we stumble through tango, both awkward and fair.
This conga of chaos, a puzzling spree,
Unraveling truths that set us free.

So take a chance, wear a silly grin,
Swaying in circles, let the fun begin.
Mysterious steps in a light-hearted chase,
Finding joy in this odd embrace!

The Pulse of Possibility

Heartbeat racing with every thrum,
A jivey rhythm, oh, look at them run!
Each step is a question, each spin a dare,
With laughter vibrating in the light summer air.

The floor is alive with uncertainty's vibe,
Can't tell if it's magic or just too much jive.
Funky moves, like jelly on toast,
Clumsy yet charming, we're here to boast.

From shimmy to shake, we test the bounds,
In this carnival of weirdness, joy abounds.
Twisting and turning our anxious fates,
In pursuit of fun, wild laughter awaits.

So let's ride this current, feel the beat rise,
Dancing through life, with wide-open eyes.
The pulse of possibility strikes up the band,
Join in the frolic, it's all so grand!

Waltz with What-Ifs

In the ballroom of choices, we sidestep fate,
With a polka of worries, don't hesitate.
What if I trip? What if I glide?
The odds don't matter, let's take a ride.

A waltz with the unknown, quirky as pie,
Every spin hatching laughter, oh my!
With "oops" and "whoops," we tango with glee,
Twisting our fates, just let it be free.

Stepping on toes, a farcical sight,
Footloose and carefree, hearts taking flight.
Under the mirrors, we glide and we sway,
Join me in chaos; let's dance this way!

So raise a toast to the dance of the strange,
As we waltz with what-ifs, anticipating change.
In the rhythm of laughter, we come alive,
This waltz is our story, let's jive and thrive!

Curves of Courage

In the kitchen, I trip on a crumb,
Twirl like a pro, not feeling so dumb.
The dog stares wide-eyed, unsure how to react,
As I cha-cha alone, finding rhythm intact.

A coffee spill, oh what a scene,
I glide and I pivot, I'm lean and I'm keen.
With each little stumble, I seem to enhance,
The choreography of my wild little dance.

The cat leaps high, in a flurry of grace,
As I jive on the floor, a smile on my face.
We're a duo of chaos, no need for a plan,
Just let the music swirl, oh what a grand slam!

So here's to the moments that life throws our way,
Where laughter's our guide, come what may.
In the quirks of the day, let our worries be gone,
As we shuffle through life, moving to our own song.

Serenade of the Spirit

The toaster pops up, and out flies two slices,
I moonwalk away, avoiding the crisis.
With butter on my foot, I slide down the hall,
It's a breakfast ballet, oh how I enthrall!

A knock on the door, oh what a surprise,
I freeze in a pose, and look through the fries.
I open it wide, in my dancewear, not neat,
The mailman just chuckles at my two left feet.

The vacuum's alive, it hums like a tune,
I tango around it, I'm quite the cartoon.
With each crazy spin, I conquer my dome,
Making messes and smiles, here in my home.

A wiggle, a giggle, the day rolls on by,
As I skip past the houseplants, I just feel so spry.
In the rhythm of life, on this comical ride,
I'll shimmy and shake, let my nonsense abide.

Embrace the Uncertainty

The clock strikes twelve, what a curious case,
I leap on the couch, give the cushions a chase.
With snacks in each hand, I'm a sight to behold,
As I boogie and bounce, feeling brave and bold.

The phone starts to ring, should I answer it now?
I shake to the beat, not following how.
With laughter and giggles, I dodge and I weave,
Celebrating the chaos, what a joy to believe.

My plants start to sway, in the breeze they all sway,
I'm the captain of joy, steering wild today.
They're my silent crew, with leaves in the air,
As I sway with abandon, without a single care.

So here's to the moments we don't understand,
Where the joy is the journey, a whimsical land.
In the dance of the day, let each twist be embraced,
For in laughter and movement, the heart is well-placed.

Twirls in the Twilight

Under a lamp's glow, the shadows all dance,
I twirl through the kitchen, not missing a chance.
The fridge hums a tune, and the blender will join,
As I waltz with the spoons—oh, the joy that I coin.

A flashlight once flickered; I leaped with a start,
A firefly's whim made me run with my heart.
Like a dervish, I spun, no need for a song,
In the chaos of twilight, everything feels wrong.

Then moonlight bursts in, and it brightens my way,
As I shimmy in circles, the night turns to play.
With stars as my audience, I laugh 'til I drop,
In the rhythm of laughter, it just doesn't stop.

So here's to the twirls, to the odd and the fun,
In the twilight's embrace, let our dances be spun.
Without fear of the fall, we'll keep making our way,
In the hilarious moments, let our spirits sway.

Liberation through Motion

In a room filled with shoes, they collide,
With moves that resemble a strange circus ride.
The cat twirls in a frantic sway,
While Grandma's rocking it in her own way.

A toddler spins, like a top on a spree,
And the dusty old lamp just shakes with glee.
The dog attempts to join the fun,
With a wiggle and jiggle, he's second to none.

A bump here, a slip—oh the giggles abound,
In this wacky realm of rhythm profound.
With every snap, clap, and silly pose,
Liberated laughter is the heartbeat's prose.

So let loose your limbs, don't hold back the cheer,
In this chaotic dance, nothing to fear.
For in every movement, you're boldly enhanced,
In the wild, quirky freedom of joyful dance.

Adrift in the Dance

Like a leaf on the breeze, we all take flight,
Wobbling and bobbling, what a funny sight.
With socks on the tile, we glide and we slide,
Laughing out loud, with no need to hide.

Cha-cha with fruit, a banana's our guide,
The kitchen turns wild, a fruity joyride.
The blender's our drummer, the toast joins the beat,
Adrift in the dance, we can't help but repeat.

Spin like a top, then tumble with grace,
Elbows flailing, we invent our own space.
Mom's got the moves, just not the right flow,
While Dad trips on air, just enjoying the show.

So gather your friends, the wackier, the better,
Let's make a dance that we won't soon forget her.
With giggles erupting, we float 'round the hall,
In this glorious chaos, we're all having a ball!

Embrace the Twists

Twist to the left, then swing to the right,
We're lost in the rhythm, what a dazzling sight.
With arms like spaghetti, we wave and we flail,
In this dance-o-sphere, we'll never derail.

The cat joins the fun, in a leap and a pounce,
With a backflip so grand, let's all take a bounce.
Dad's doing the worm, it's a sight to behold,
While Grandma's breakdancing, so brave and so bold.

The pizza rolls by with a jig and a shake,
As the chorus of laughter, our hearts gently quake.
With a duck and a dive, we all join the fun,
In this wiggly world, together we run.

So don't take a seat; keep moving your feet,
The magic of motion can't ever be beat.
Just embrace the twists, let your worries unwind,
In this funny dance, all your laughs you will find.

Footfalls of Freedom

The floor's an adventure, come skip and hop,
With mismatched socks, let your wildness crop.
Each step makes a sound, a clink and a clang,
In this dance of delight, hear the laughter hang.

A shake of the shoulders, a bounce to the beat,
The rhythm unfolds, it can't be discreet.
We'll cha-cha with chairs, tango with the broom,
In the footfalls of freedom, there's always room.

No majestic ballet, no grandeur in sight,
Just silly old moves, every step feels so right.
With friends all around, we dodge and we weave,
In this kooky escapade, you'll never believe.

So kick up your heels, let the giggles ring wide,
In the dance of the carefree, we'll never subside.
For joy's found in motion, let's lure it out hence,
In our footfalls of freedom, let's make some pretense!

The Ballet of Bravery

In a tutu made of bubble wrap,
I prance upon a crooked map.
My pirouette takes quite a twist,
I'm twirling through a random mist.

With confidence like wobbly clay,
I leap and bounce in disarray.
A grand jeté on slippery floors,
I'm dodging doubts and open doors.

The audience is just my cat,
Who thinks this dance is quite the spat.
With every step, I laugh and spin,
In my ballet, there's no such sin.

So here I go, I take the stage,
Lord help me, I'm quite the page!
In a world that makes no sense,
A little dance? It's pure suspense!

Tap Dance Through Turmoil

I shuffle left, then tap my shoe,
With rhythms that are far from true.
Life's a beat I cannot find,
But tapping helps, it's my own kind.

With every clack, I shake my fears,
The floor is roaring, loud and clear.
I dance my way through clumsy strife,
Jake from State Farm claps for life.

Step, slide, then spin around,
Lost my keys, but still I'm sound.
A dance-off with my laundry pile,
I jest through chaos with a smile.

So if you're lost amidst the mess,
Don't fret, just wear your tap shoe dress!
The clattering drum of life will cheer,
A funny jig to bring good cheer!

Spin into the Great Uncertainty

Round and round, like dizzy bees,
I spin my doubts into the breeze.
What's left or right I cannot choose,
But hey, at least I've got my shoes.

With blindfolds on, I whirl and sway,
Commentators say, "What a display!"
They giggle loud, but I don't mind,
In circles, all my woes unwind.

The world is whirling, quite absurd,
"Where's the exit?" I preferred.
Yet as I spin, I feel the thrill,
A dizzy dance negates the chill.

So here's my twirl, a wild charade,
Through uncertain times, I parade.
Just keep on spinning, let it flow,
You'll find your feet—eventually, though!

Rhythm of the Indecisive

Should I cha-cha or do the twist?
The choices leave me quite bemused.
I hop from folk to disco flair,
A merry mix beyond compare.

One step forward, then I retreat,
Lost in the groove of my own beat.
A little jig, a shimmy shake,
I balance life like a cupcake.

With side-to-sides, I go astray,
What's next? Even I can't say!
Yet limbs are flinging, spirits high,
Dancing frets just wave goodbye!

So loss of path? A laughing jest,
In every step, I give my best.
Embrace the chaos, shake it free,
In the rhythm of my mystery!

Flicker of Adventure

In a world of wobbling feet,
I twirl like a clumsy kite.
Around me, laughter flits,
As I dance through day and night.

The floor is a trampoline,
I leap and somersault high.
Do I look like a gazelle?
More like a confused pie!

With each awkward shuffle,
Joy spills from every grin.
Who cares if I stumble?
Life's a jest, and I'm in!

So I shimmy and shake,
In this zany ballet.
Embrace the silly tunes,
And let them lead the way!

Embrace the Paradox

Like a chicken on a hot plate,
I flap and lose my place.
In the whirl of fumbles,
I stumble with a smiley face.

The rhythm of chaos calls,
Here I bounce, there I sway.
Uncertain of my moves,
Yet I boogie without delay!

Fortune favors the goofy,
I'll trip, then hop, then slide.
Twists of fate are a delight,
In this silly, crazy ride.

So if you're feeling askew,
Just follow my lead, my friend.
Let's laugh through the missteps,
And make the odd moments blend!

Dance of the Spirit's Query

Wobble and twirl, I reset,
Questions in the air like confetti.
With every goofy spin,
My heart flips like spaghetti.

The music plays a riddle,
What's right, what's a bit wrong?
Who cares when I can jiggle,
To this upbeat, quirky song?

My body becomes a jester,
Filling the room with cheer.
Not knowing the next step,
Is half the fun, I cheer!

So let's dance and chuckle,
While spirals swirl around.
In this teeter-totter of life,
Joy is where we're bound!

Trust the Tempo

In a room full of giggles, I start to groove,
My feet are a riddle, but I still move.
Twisting and turning, like spaghetti on a plate,
Who needs good judgment? I'll just be late.

A two-step stumble, a shuffle and spin,
My moves are all silly, but oh what a win!
Laughter erupts as I trip and glide,
A dance floor disaster, but I'm filled with pride.

So I kick off my shoes, embrace sheer delight,
Feet tapping thunder, under disco lights.
No rhythm's required, just joy in the air,
Let's wiggle and wobble, without a care.

With each chuckle and slip, my spirit does fly,
Not quite a ballerina, but I aim for the sky.
So grab a partner, let's frolic about,
In this whirlwind of funny, let's twist and shout!

Spirited Steps

With a hop and a skip, I take to the floor,
Jazz hands at the ready, who knows what's in store?
I may look ridiculous, but that's the fun call,
Each bounce and twist, I'm having a ball.

Fumbling my way through a cha-cha parade,
My feet feel like jelly and yet I'm not swayed.
A wiggle, a jiggle, I think I'm in tune,
The cats and the dogs must be howling at the moon.

Grab your neighbor, watch our wild affair,
Spinning in circles, we're floating on air.
As I trip over nothing, I find my own beat,
Who knew clumsy chaos could feel so sweet?

So if life's got you stunned, or feeling a mess,
Just launch into motion, and let out that stress.
With laughter in troves and spirit untamed,
In this quirky ballet, nobody's shamed.

Uncharted Choreography

In the middle of the crowd, I claim my own space,
With moves so absurd, it's a slapstick race.
I swish and I swoosh, like a wayward kite,
A flail here or there, oh what a sight!

With confidence high, I attempt the moonwalk,
But it feels more like a misfit's awkward squawk.
Now I'm sliding and gliding, with flair on display,
Each shake and shimmy blows worries away.

A conga line brews, with folks in a whirl,
We bump into table, and give it a twirl.
Forget all the rules; we're creating our game,
These uncharted steps, we'll all share the fame.

Life's less of a ball, and more of a rave,
Each chuckle and tumble, a memory we save.
So let the world watch, let them pause and stare,
In this goofy ballet, we float on air.

Serene Sway

When the beat drops low, and the room spins around,
I take a deep breath, and let the rhythm surround.
Arms flailing freely, like wind in the trees,
A giggle escapes as I dance with the breeze.

With a sway to the left and a bob to the right,
I'm lost in the moment, feeling just right.
No steps to perfection, just chaos and flair,
With joy in the shuffle, we're dancing on air.

So if you see me wobble, just know I'm at peace,
Every clumsy encounter brings laughter's release.
Join in the merriment, don't be afraid,
In this world of absurdity, let's enjoy the parade!

For in every misstep, there's a smile to find,
In the dance of the unsure, we leave thought behind.
So come as you are, and let the world sway,
In each slip and stumble, we find our own way.

Waltz Among the Questions

Twirl around the whims of thought,
Where answers hide, and doubts are caught.
Step on toes, and laugh out loud,
In this chaos, feel so proud.

Clumsy feet, but so much flair,
Who needs rhythm? We just dare.
With every spin, a giggle grows,
Life's a dance, as everyone knows.

Jumping with Doubt

Skip through hurdles, leap over fears,
With a hop and a grin that cheers.
Bouncing on whims, what a sight,
Doubt can't dim this wild delight.

Jump so high, the ground feels far,
Falling's like dance, a spontaneous star.
Land with a flourish, what a show,
Celebrate each misstep, let it flow.

A Dance Through Shadows

Sway to the whispers of the night,
Shadows giggle, giving fright.
Stumble here, and bounce right there,
Every misstep's a laugh to share.

In the dark, who needs to find?
Just shimmy on, don't fall behind.
Lift up your feet, and glide with glee,
Don't mind the specters, just be free!

Grace in the Face of Confusion

Flutter like leaves in a whimsical breeze,
Confusion reigns, but it's sure to please.
Wobble and twirl, embrace the funk,
With each odd twist, we'll laugh and clunk.

Ballet or breakdance? It matters not,
Just sway and sashay, connect the dot.
In this frenzy, we find our might,
Grace is a giggle in the spotlight.

Grace in the Unknown

Twirl like a dervish, lose all your cares,
Stumble on laughter, forget all your flares.
Giddy in motion, with toes out of line,
Slip on a banana, say 'Isn't that fine?'

Step into shadows, chase after the light,
Bump into strangers who dance out of sight.
Fumbles and giggles, the rhythm's your friend,
Every wild misstep is a reason to blend.

Moves That Mend the Mind

Jiggle like jelly, let loose with a grin,
Wobble like noodles, let silliness in.
Each pirouette, a tickle is found,
The brain's in a whirl, but who holds it down?

Avoiding the worries that swirl in the air,
Mimic a chicken—that's wonderful flair!
Laugh off the doubts like they're shoes made of glue,
With each silly spin, embrace something new.

Chaotic Harmony

Shuffling and sliding, a fine mess we weave,
Jigs turned to jumbles, like socks left to grieve.
Forget about rhythm, let chaos be king,
Jump with the jester, and hear the heart sing!

Round and around, what a ruckus we make,
Mix salsa with waltz, the floor starts to quake.
Swirl up the madness, let it all flow,
In the whirl of the silly, we're all in the show.

Revelry Amid the Riddle

Baffled by puzzles and glazed with surprise,
The answers may hide in the way that one flies.
Skip like a frog on a pogo stick spree,
Unravel the riddle with hops full of glee!

So twist and turn while you puzzle it out,
Forget all your worries, let laughter sprout.
In the dance of confusion, the joy we will find,
With every wild move, we expand our own mind.

Tango of the Torn

In the midst of a whirl, I trip on my shoe,
A dance so absurd, the floor feels brand new.
With each awkward step, I'm lost in the beat,
Who knew that two left feet could feel so sweet?

A spin brings a stumble, I'm laughing out loud,
While onlookers whisper, 'Is he in a crowd?'
Yet my heart does the tango, it knows how to sway,
In a world of chaos, I'll lead the ballet!

Fumbling Toward Joy

I twirl and I twist, arms flailing in space,
With joy in my heart, I embrace the disgrace.
A shuffle and shuffle, I'm lost in my groove,
Each step is a giggle, I'm starting to move.

Step forward, then back, it's a curious sight,
Like a chicken in heels, I'm dancing with might.
My laughter erupts like confetti in air,
Who cares if I'm clumsy? I'm free like a hare!

Shadows of Serenity

The floor is a stage, with shadows that play,
Each movement I make, lights guide the way.
A moonwalk in slippers, a glide through the night,
Falling, I'm flying, it all feels so right.

With balletic twists, like a sock on a cat,
I twirl with abandon, not caring where I'm at.
In the chaos of rhythm, I find my release,
And dance like a dervish, my spirit's caprice!

Leaps into the Abyss

I leap into nothing, with a heart full of glee,
Who knows what awaits, but hey, it's just me!
With arms all akimbo and a grin on my face,
I plunge with a wiggle, I'll find my own place.

A twist and a turn, oh what a grand fall,
Each flounder enticing, I'm loving it all.
The abyss may be waiting, but I'm having fun,
No need for perfection, I'm dancing as one!

www.ingramcontent.com/pod-product-compliance
Lightning Source LLC
Chambersburg PA
CBHW072149200426
43209CB00051B/983